INFP: A Flower in the Shade

By Sandra Nichols

INFP's are Romantic Heroes who endow the world with their healing energy. This book is dedicated to them.

Table of Contents

Introduction

Each human being is a unique creation of individuality. His abilities, motivations, and values characterize his distinctiveness. The conditions of his environment, his life experiences and his biological origins influence his ability to adapt to the world and effect the manner in which he grows and develops. The way a person views his world and how he makes sense of it, however, is dependent upon basic mental functions that come naturally to him. For example, he has a preference for acquiring his energy from either the introverted, inner world of ideas, or the extraverted, outer world of people and things. He also has a preference for perceiving through the use of either his sensing ability or his intuition. His method for coming to decisions and judging matters is based on either his thoughts or his emotions. An additional mental aspect has to do with his approach to life which is either one of a structured lifestyle or one that is basically unstructured in nature.

The preference for either extraversion or introversion, the manner in which a person perceives and makes judgments, and his preference for either a structured or an unstructured lifestyle, create what is known in psychology as the personality type. Personality defines what makes individuals different. Although each human being is exceptional, there are similarities shared by certain groups of people whose fundamental thought patterns are very much alike. Their personal interests, needs, and motivations are unique to their type and their characteristics are often similar.

Personality type has been studied extensively by psychologists. The eminent Swiss psychiatrist, Carl G. Jung (1875 – 1961), first introduced the theory. In his work entitled "Psychological Types", Jung asserted that individuals have natural patterns for taking in information and making decisions. He also developed the idea of extraversion and introversion which he called the attitudes. The extraverted person derives his energy from the outer world of people and things whereas the introverted person derives his energy from the inner world of ideas. Jung further described four basic mental functions of the human mind--intuition, sensing, feeling and thinking. Jung's personality theory consisted of eight possible combinations of the two attitudes and four mental functions, resulting in eight types of distinctly different personalities.

Jung's work has had the greatest influence on personality theory, prompting the development of various personality type assessments based on his work. The Myers-Briggs Type Indicator® (MBTI®) is the most prevalent one. The MBTI® is based on the extensive research of personality types conducted by Isabel Briggs Myers (1897-1980) and her mother, Katharine C. Briggs (1875-1968). These remarkable women, whose work began in the 1920's, developed a framework for the identification of personality types, based on Jung's theories. Myers and Briggs incorporated the introversion and extraversion attitudes of Jung as well as his four mental functions of sensing, intuition, thinking, and feeling and added a fourth dichotomy for perception and judgment. The resulting MBTI® is a questionnaire that classifies personalities into sixteen unique types.

The Myers-Briggs Type Indicator® was published in 1962. The personality assessment is a comprehensible and practical tool for interpreting Jung's psychological principles and is the most popular personality assessment used today. The questionnaire helps individuals to develop to their full potential by appreciating what Myers referred to as their "Gifts Differing" in her famous 1980 book by that name. The profiles give individuals an opportunity to examine their true nature from a psychological perspective and to appreciate their difference, as well as their unique talents and life challenges.

When studying personality types, perception and judgment are the basic mental functions explored. Perception involves how one views or becomes aware of his world. There are two ways of perceiving something. People primarily use either their senses or their intuition. Although the brain is capable of using both the senses and intuition, of course, there is a strong impulse for the use of one mental function over the other; one is either naturally predisposed to viewing the world by sensing or by using intuition. An individual's preference for perceiving with the senses or with intuition is rather easy to distinguish by one's behavior. The sensing person likes to use his five senses to directly observe what is around him while an intuitive person prefers to imagine the possibilities of things by making associations and formulating ideas about meaning or potential. A sensing person uses a hands-on approach to acquire an understanding of the physical reality of a situation. The person using intuition forms a sense of the symbolic nature of the situation, the bigger picture of its significance.

The aptitude for either sensing or intuition is inborn; children start to show signs of their preference as they begin to relate to the world around them. They become skilled at their preferences because either of the sensing or intuitive ability proves to be more reliable, enjoyable and useful for them. A child's preference also draws him to activities that allow use of his perceptual disposition. For example, the child who prefers use of the senses will enjoy activities that allow him to touch, feel, see and hear, while the child whose mind prefers intuition will be drawn to very different activities that allow him to dream, create, and imagine what might be.

In their inventory, Myers and Briggs used a four-letter acronym for each of the sixteen personality types, such as the INFP personality about whom this book is written. The second letter in the Myers-Briggs acronym refers to the perceiving preference already discussed and is either represented by S for the sensing preference or the letter N for the preference for intuition. INFP personality types perceive using their intuition, which is represented by the letter N in INFP. The INFP's exhibit a keen sense of just knowing that something is so and they have an affinity for comprehending abstract concepts, making associations, and considering possibilities.

Individuals also have a preferred way of judging what they perceive. Judging is the function of the mind that determines how one makes decisions. People prefer to use thinking or feeling for this mental process. The judging tendency is often obvious to observers because the difference in behavior between thinking and feeling types is quite apparent. As with perception, individuals are capable of both ways of judging—by using their thinking or their feeling attributes. However, personality typing identifies the *preferred* or predominantly used manner of judging. When someone makes a decision by thinking, he examines the details, studies the facts, or gathers relevant details. When someone bases decisions on feelings, he thinks about how a situation may affect people. The judging preference is the third letter of the Myers-Briggs acronym. Thinking types are represented by the letter T and feeling types by the letter F. The INFP judges using his feeling preference, which is the letter F in INFP. He is the most compassionate of all the types and makes his decisions based upon how things will impact people.

So far, four mental functions have been explained: perceiving by using sensing (S) or intuition (N) and judging by using thinking (T) or feeling (F). These mental functions are natural tendencies that influence one's external behavior. For example, faced with engine difficulty, a thinker may develop a plan based on the facts associated with the mechanical problem, such as the distance to the nearest garage, the availability of his tools, and so forth. If he is also a sensing type, he'll have his head under the hood to diagnose the problem, smelling what is burning up, feeling for a burst pipe, or looking for a disconnected wire. The feeling type passenger in the car might be focused more on how upset her boss will be when she is late for her meeting. If she's also an intuitive, she may be thinking of the possibilities for preventing future engine failures with proper periodic maintenance and might appear aloof about the delay because she has an unconscious awareness that her friend under the hood knows what he's doing and there is nothing to worry about because he'll soon fix the problem.

To review, there are two preferences for perceiving: sensing or intuition, and two preferences for judging, thinking or feeling. In Myers-Briggs typing, the perceiving and judging abbreviations are combined for each individual. There are sensing and thinking types (ST), sensing and feeling types (SF), intuitive and thinking types (NT) and intuitive and feeling types (NF), such as the INFP. Behavior is greatly influenced by these pairs of preferences. The contrasts and their combinations are part of what make people unique. But that is not all. There is an additional natural tendency with which humans are graced. It involves the extraversion and introversion attitude originated by Carl Jung. This preference is represented by the first letter of the Myers-Briggs type acronym.

Jung's psychological theory of extraversion and introversion has been modified since its origin in the 1920's. In personality typing, the extravert or introvert preference defines the inherent tendency to prefer either the external or internal environment. It is described by Myers as where one obtains his energy. Extraversion is the preference for the outer world of actuality; introversion is the preference for the inner world of ideas. At a basic level, extraverts like to be among people and things and introverts prefer to be alone and private. Extraverts are expressive, whereas, introverts are more reserved. Extraverts are outgoing by nature while introverts are more unrevealing. The difference between these two mental functions is easy to detect, but only if the preference is being used, for one may easily act *as if* he is extraverted or introverted. Although an introvert like the INFP has the capacity to act like an extravert, for example, he has a strong predilection and enjoyment for introversion because he is more comfortable in his inner world. Extraversion and introversion are not a measure of one's vitality. They describe the environment within which individuals are at their best and where they feel more at ease.

The inclination for extraversion or introversion will determine, to a great extent, the type of activities one enjoys, the interests he has, the nature of his relationships, and where he feels motivated. The attitude is reflected in a host of character traits as well. Extraversion is symbolized with E and Introversion with I, in typing terms. They are the first letter of the Myers-Briggs personality acronym. Eight possible personalities have now been identified: IST, ISF, ENT, INT, EST, ESF, ENF, and INF. The remaining, fourth letter completes the profile and has to do with how one responds to his world.

Myers and Briggs added the final dichotomy to the Jungian theories--the judging or perceiving function, indicated by the letters J or P. This function is represented by the last letter of the MBTI acronym. Of course, this preference is a bit confusing because the middle letters are also about the perceiving and judging preferences. The fourth letter, however, describes how an individual behaves in the outside world. He either makes a definitive conclusion about something in a structured manner (judging) or remains open to its possibilities (perceiving). Judging types like to arrive at a yes/no, like/don't like, approve/disapprove determination quickly and firmly. Perceiving types like to ponder different angles and possibilities carefully before making a decision. It is easy to see how behavior differs between judgers and perceivers. Judgers like it cut and dried. Perceivers give things more time and consideration. The INFP personality is a perceiving type. He likes to "go with the flow" rather than having a structured lifestyle or set schedule.

As an example of the judging or perceiving aptitude, both types may receive a party invitation that includes an RSVP card. The two personalities will probably respond to the invitation in different ways based on their preferences. The judging type may make his decision quickly, complete his response, and return the RSVP to the sender the very day of its delivery to him in the mail. He might file the invitation appropriately in a folder designated for similar correspondence. He enjoys structure, order, planning, and schedule. By contrast, the perceiving type, such as the INFP, may take his time with the RSVP and possibly put it aside for later while he considers the consequences of his RSVP acceptance or declination. He may give a great deal of thought to how his decision will affect others. He may not have a designated place for such correspondence and may have difficulty finding the card a week later when he realizes his response is due. The perceiving type considers the possibilities from a number of angles and doesn't need things to be cut and dried.

The final letter J (judging) or P (perceiving) completes the personality acronym used in Myers-Briggs typing. There are 16 possible four-letter combinations defined by the inventory, meaning each person has one of sixteen possible Myers-Briggs type personalities. Each one of the types is unique and they are equal in terms of their importance. No one type is better than the other. Although each personality is capable of behaving in his non-dominant manner, such as when an introverted person plays an extraverted role, or when one who prefers feeling attitudes thinks about facts and details, by and large, there are inborn, indisputably natural tendencies that every normal individual prefers and enjoys. (The reference to "normal" is intended to mean normal brain function that is not impeded by illness). The INFP is the subject of this book. He is Introverted, perceives with his intuitive ability, judges by using his feelings, and conducts his life perceptively.

For the INFP, the opposing aspects of his personality are the sensing and thinking functions. In terms of his natural preference, they are secondary mental functions for his type. They are somewhat immature, though they are called to action when necessary and can become quite skilled during the course of his life. For example, the INFP will certainly need to use his less developed sensing skills to assemble a chest of drawers from IKEA, instead of relying completely on his intuition, for obvious reasons. This does not mean to say that his intuitive ability is not used during the process. It simply means that the sensing skills predominate on a temporary basis because they are more effective in accomplishing the task. Similarly, he may need to replace his feeling capacity with his thinking mind, at times, to solve a complex problem involving logic. He is not as adept at the thinking function as a thinking type for this particular activity, however, he is capable of adapting to situations that require the thinking function when needed on a temporary basis.

For each of the sixteen types, one of the two middle letters representing the perceiving and judging preferences is considered the dominant process that takes the lead. For the INFP, it is feeling, which is a judging preference. Intuition, the perceiving preference, is the INFP's subordinate function. The dominance of his feeling preference accounts for many of his behaviors, values, motivations, interests, and also his problems. He is greatly concerned about the human condition and is benevolent in nature. He is friendly toward others and concerned about their welfare.

David Keirsey,(1921 – 2013), an American psychologist who developed the Keirsey Temperament Sorter personality questionnaire and who authored the two internationally best-selling editions of *Please Understand Me*, grouped the personalities somewhat differently than Myers and Briggs. Keirsey's basic premise, however, was gleaned from the works of Carl Jung and Isabel Myers. Unlike Myers, who concentrated on the psychological functions, Keirsey asserted in his work that temperament is based more on the observable characteristics of a person such as his habits and behavior. Based on these behaviors, he defined four temperaments—the Rationals, Artisans, Guardians, and Idealists. He described the four temperaments in terms of the way they used words and tools. According to his theory, words are used either in a concrete or abstract manner and tools are used either cooperatively or based on utility. He explained that INFP's are in the Idealist temperament group; they use words abstractly and they use tools cooperatively.

Keirsey further described each of the four temperaments as having roles and role variants. The Idealists' roles, for example, were either that of Mentors or Advocates. The role of the INFP is that of Advocate. Keirsey's role variants for the Advocates were the Teachers, Counselors, Champions, and Healers. In Keirsey's terms, INFP Advocates have the role variant of the Healer. So, according to Keirsey, INFP's are Idealists, Advocates and Healers. INFP's care deeply about helping to make improvements, both for people and things. Isabel Myers herself was an INFP devoted to helping people discover their unique gifts as a means of improving their self-awareness and enjoyment of life. Other famous INFP's include Princess Diana, Helen Keller, and Audrey Hepburn.

Unlike Jung and Myers, whose functional theories described the workings of the mind, Keirsey's focus was more on observable behavior. In particular, he described objectively what he considered the most developed and intelligent action among the types, meaning their most useful and effective traits. Another difference in the theories of Myers and Keirsey involves their hypotheses on the extent to which the personalities are integrated. Psychologically speaking, for Myers, the elements of the personality must become integrated during the course of life; Keirsey asserted that the personalities are already integrated. They become what they are meant to be and the process by which that happens is not through intentional efforts to integrate the different preferences but from the natural course of maturation.

The insights of Carl Jung, Isabel Myers, Katharine Briggs, and David Keirsey are alike in fundamental ways. Their theories, overall, provide a means of viewing personality difference systematically. Each of these scholars described how the personalities differ, how they manage their lives, how they progress and how they relate to one another. Learning about one's own profile can help an individual who is in search of greater self-awareness because it provides a perspective that rings true for him about his nature and explains the behavior, challenges, and personal problems unique to his personality. Knowledge of personality type illuminates the positive aspects and strengths of one's personality and illustrates them as the gifts they truly are. Everyone has special gifts and life is more fulfilling when individuals respect their own attributes and those of others. To learn how and why individuals behave as they do, how they perceive their world in a unique way, and what truly motivates them is a means of separating fact from fiction and can help greatly in understanding the true self. It is also a means of learning why the negative aspects of personality emerge. Understanding one's type also leads to an awareness that the personality disguises one wears at times are temporary alterations that do not have the capacity to threaten an individual's authenticity.

For over seventy years, the science behind the MBTI® is unchanged. The personality types created by the Myers and Briggs theory in the 1940's still define what is innately unique about individuals, no matter when, where or how they may have been raised or what life situations they may have encountered. The profiles define the very essence of human personality. The result of the Jungian personality assessments are reliable, no matter the age or stage of life at which they may be taken because the tendencies that come naturally to individuals represent their true core. Although everyone is capable of adaptations that require the use of their subordinate preferences or the opposite aspects of their personalities, they will always feel more at ease with their preferences because they are instinctive and natural. One's preferences do not change throughout the course of life, no matter what may occur during a lifetime.

The Myers-Briggs Type Indicator® continues to be a reliable assessment of personality types, defining the means by which individuals perceive the world and how they arrive at decisions. The MBTI® was initially a scholarly pursuit. When published in 1975 by the Consulting Psychologist Press, its use became widespread. Keirsey's Temperament Sorter, was also developed in the 1970's. Both personality type assessment tools are taken by millions of people each year. They continue to be dependable resources for individual and team development internationally. Counselors, therapists, and consultants consider them to be accurate and effective ways for their patients and clients to understand personality difference. The testing is used to help individuals achieve self-awareness and to learn how to deal with personal problems unique to their type. In group settings and companies, the assessments provide a helpful foundation for team building, organizational management and conflict resolution. The therapeutic benefit of psychological typing in group environments is primarily that of learning about the differences among work teams, how to effectively get along together and respect one another's individuality.

The typology scholars were intuitive, in personality typology terms. Their remarkable observations of human behavior and their ability to formulate a conceptual analysis of the personality dichotomies is evidence of intuitive intelligence at its best. They developed scholarly perspectives of personality that can be used as therapeutic resources for personal guidance. Their work helps to explain the underlying reasons for human behavior unique to each individual. Personality typing is immensely popular among laypeople. It is not pop psychology, however, nor is it New Age philosophy. It is a time-honored, statistically valid theory that explains difference and that helps people identify their place in the world. These scholars have bequeathed to the world, a starting point for achieving self-knowledge and self-acceptance, life balance, purpose, and fulfillment.

Personalities are fundamentally different. In order to feel good about themselves and others, people must come to an appreciation of difference by taking the time to understand and respect diversity. There is no point in trying to change anyone's inherent preferences because it simply cannot be done. If a person finds someone else's behavior annoying or intolerable, that person is probably an opposite type, one with whom he will never share similar ways of seeing the world or responding to it. However, he can learn to understand and respect his own difference and that of those unlike him. A judging personality type, for example, who cannot understand the perceiving friend's disinterest in routine or schedules may as well save his breath if he tries to convince his perceiving type friend to establish a structured lifestyle. His friend is indeed capable of change on a temporary basis, but he will always revert to the preferred style and related behavior because it is simply more natural for him to do so. In fact, anyone can change traits, but those adaptations are impermanent and can never threaten the preservation of the true, underlying personality.

An understanding of one's own values, ambitions, and vulnerabilities leads to a more contented life. Personality profiles help people by identifying the pure essence of the self that exists behind masks of social convention or neurotic tendencies. When the authentic nature is concealed by these psychological forces, an individual is not entirely at peace. Quite often, emotional problems can be addressed by considering the extent to which the true self may simply be crying for its liberation. When one discovers his gifts differing, in essence, he discovers his truth which can be an enlightening and therapeutic process that restores self-confidence and a sense of self-worth. There are many psychological insecurities that impede man's celebration of his authentic self. When there is acceptance of the *true* nature, one learns to appreciate his difference, including the less-developed aspects of his personality, and this discovery can make him feel less threatened by his limitations. Understanding personality type is a means of becoming aware of one's greatest potentialities and purpose. Discovering the true and, perhaps, oppressed nature is not merely intellectually enlightening; it can help an individual understand how to seek enjoyment in life, to learn what predisposes him to certain emotional problems and to address his challenges more effectively. When type is considered comprehensively, for its intended purpose--to understand deeply how one thinks, feels, behaves, and differs, a person learns that he is okay.

If the result of the Myers-Briggs Type Indicator® is the INFP personality, typology experts define him as the Healer, the Mediator, the Romantic, or the Advocate. He is all of those things, in fact. The INFP is one of the rarest types, representing only about one or two percent of the population. He is an idealist who focuses on needs and thinks about how to make improvements and he thinks about that most of the time. It was Keirsey who called the INFP's the Healers. Their dominant feeling preference and, in particular, their compassion, is the impetus for the value they place on causes and needs. They are empathic to the point of selflessness; they truly care about the wellbeing of everyone and the improvement of everything, and they believe in goodness as the inherent and prevailing nature of mankind. They value truth and self-growth. The INFP's are private individuals who are sensitive, diplomatic, reserved, flexible, and cooperative.

Non-idealists types—what Keirsey called the Artisans, Guardians, and Rationals, often find the Healer difficult to understand. They may describe him as aloof or unrealistic. He is not. The inner world of INFP's is alive with activity and their hearts are full of compassion. They hold tremendous promise for the world and have a gift of unifying that which has broken apart. Their energy may *appear* to be subdued; however, their enthusiasm for the ideals they value is extraordinary. To understand their true gifts is to know their immense energy. They are romantic individualists who advocate for causes dear to them. They are healers with a special gift for comprehending the big picture and the abstract. With these unique gifts, they are capable of making associations within complex systems and of creating holistic visions and imagery. They are naturally skilled in bringing things and people together, healing separations with their compassion and their intuitive knowledge.

Keirsey adored the Idealists. He thought they were like dolphins, because of their cooperative, gentle nature, their nurturing parental style, their friendliness with people, and their close family ties. These INFP traits are manifestations of the INFP's compassion, the depth of which makes them endearing souls. They have a delightful ability to identify, seek, and achieve wholeness. To the INFP's, authenticity is everything—what is at the heart of a thing or a person, in other words, its truth. They are less concerned with the details than the thinking types are, for they are feeling-dominant. INFP's recognize the power of love as the ultimate form of healing. They delight at the prospect of romance in all its glorious forms. In their peace-keeping style of life, they are the mediators who adapt extremely well to situations they do not feel comfortable in because they value harmonious relationships. As long as something meets with their moral standards, the INFP's are remarkably flexible.

INFP's possess an awareness that is instinctive and spontaneous. They are futurists who envision that a better world is possible through individual awareness. They are also wonderful writers. Famous authors of this type include George Orwell, Virginia Wolfe, C.S. Lewis, Franz Kafka, Edgar Allan Poe, and Shakespeare. Their work is poetic, lyrical, and romantic, and they have an outstanding gift of metaphor.

An INFP is dedicated to self-knowledge. In fact, in his two editions of *Please Understand Me,* Keirsey maintained that the INFP wants more than any other type to achieve self-actualization. Learning the intricacies of his type can help him

The INFP is a romantic hero in many ways. His issues and causes are fundamentally the same as the revolutionary social outcasts of the late 18th century. He values the freedom of the individual to be his authentic self and he strives to fend off forces that threaten personal freedom. The INFP protests against the same inhibiting cultural forces of the romantic period: constraint, social order, conformity, orthodoxy, oppression, and personal limitation. They are the very obstructions that arouse his nostalgic longing and his quest for truth. He fantasizes the ideal; he creates the imagery that symbolizes the need for more beauty and peace in the world and for the recognition of one's worth and autonomy. INFP's are as likely to advocate for the same social causes as the romantic revolutionaries of history. They protest against the subjugation of autonomy. They are humanitarians devoted to a philosophy of goodness and peacekeeping and they seek to claim the freedom they need for executing their work.

During the Romantic era, preservation of individuality and freedom of expression were evident in new forms of art and defended in political discussion with great emotional intensity. Recognition of the self and self-consciousness emerged at that time. Rationalism was slapped in the face with primordial expression in art forms. The Romantics did what the INFP who needs to release his creative energy must do—they burst into flame with passion in defense of their truths. Rebellious INFP's need to express their ideas in the same manner whenever their passion is stifled. When they are constrained by the culture, when they are selfless for too long, when they feel unappreciated, or when they find a worthy cause that ignites their compassion, they need to find a means of expressing their objections in defense of their truths or enthusiastically champion a cause. When they do, they share their gift of healing in a unique and awe-inspiring manner.

The INFP must write, sing, compose, draw, sculpt, craft, counsel or otherwise create the imagery of his inner turmoil with his hands, his mind, his voice or his heart. With the release of his enslaved spirit, always dutifully abiding and mindful of others, caring and giving, he opens the floodgates to his power. He may win the battle for autonomy in the trenches of the culture, arguing for the rules to change or imploring for modification of systems in a board room. He may express his objections against cruelties or inhumanity with his art or his counsel. Whatever his craft, he must champion a cause at some level with the innate strength of his healing talents. Like the Romantic hero, he thrives when he lets his emotions ignite simmering resentment into something of strange and romantic beauty that he alone can create.

The contributions of the Romantics of any era is to provide the culture with a new lens through which to view the world and that is exactly what the INFP does. In the Romantic Period, it was the threat of social, political, and cultural changes of the time that spawned the movement. The Romantic writers abandoned traditional literary conventions and introduced new genres and styles in their writing. The mystical, the lyrical, the provocative literary styles of the Romantic Era appealed with sentiment to idealistic values. The individual was central and the emotions of its composers, musicians, artists, architects and writers poured forth with boldness, and poignancy. It was emotional realism that marked the art of the time. The world was growing out of control and the essence of that which was inherently good was threatened. It was a massive INFP-style rally of intervention, a romantic revolution.

Romantics opposed the new way of logical and scientific thinking. They feared the impact of these changes on the human condition. Their art reflected the need to preserve wholeness, spirituality, and nature. For these reasons, there was a resurgence of interest in medieval times and Shakespearean verse. Their nostalgia was generated as a defense of the purity and truth they believed was at risk of destruction. Nostalgia is a mystical memory for romantics, a powerful force of both melancholy and comfort simultaneously. The resurrection of their past was their escape from a fated future. Romantic heroes, rejected by society, opposed its conventions and escaped to the inner world of introspection and when their fury of dissension emerged, the world watched and listened in awe. The same sense of alienation, of opposition, and of romance is inherent in the INFP. The same poignancy is evident in his work and his energy when he is inspired.

The Romantic Era was a time of intense emotion and imagery that reflected a heightened appreciation of universal truths. It was the bursting of unbridled, creative spirit in defense of freedom. The Romantics were separatists, outcasts of society who advocated for ideals with their depictions of the strange and the sublime, of fantasy and of horror. Their art embodied themes inherent in the INFP personality—individualism, independence, appreciation of nature, the self, truth, and beauty. Yet, for all the depth of its sensitivity, and its exquisite contributions still evident today, historians admit that romanticism was a complex and indefinable period, much like the INFP personality itself. Who but an idealist can truly identify with the dark romanticism of Edgar Allan Poe, or the sweet melancholy of a John Keats poem? Who but the INFP asserts that the depth of his imagery is inscrutable to the mainstream?

Romance for the INFP is not simply a preference for the fanciful or for candlelight and love making. It is an imperative of life. It is a need for eternal truths that are beyond comprehension by the rational mind. It is a desire for incorporating those truths into his days in an effort to transform the mundane life and to preserve purity and its longevity so critical to survival and to the enlightenment of the self. To the romantic INFP, the essence of love and beauty is real. To him, the discovery of its forms is the purpose of life itself. To him, the greatest pleasure is in the discovery of romantic ideals and he purposely steps outside the conformity of culture precisely to find it. In the world of rules, he rebels for the sake of his individuality and thus removes the barriers to his eccentricity. For his peace of mind, the INFP must escape the forces that threaten his liberty to express himself. He is a romantic rebel who suffers when he cannot be one.

The INFP escapes to the world of dreams and imagination where there are no boundaries. In peace, he liberates his soul with powerful emotion and produces the strange, the bizarre, and the radical. This is imaginative treason against the slavery of the human soul. He escapes the bondage of conventionality with his craft of expression and creativity in order to heal his wounded heart and free his soul from captivity. The world has the INFP's to thank for visceral forms of expression, heroic demonstrations of courage that challenge the status quo with their verse, their canvas, their words, or simply with their charm.

INFP's whose love of metaphor in unsurpassed by any type is, himself, a metaphor of the Romantic Hero. Romantic surroundings soothe him. He is the rare and delicate shade flower who often feels alienated and yearns for love. His environment must be conducive to romance with elements of nature and beauty. He seeks lovingness in everyone. He overlooks the shortcomings of a partner, in favor of seeking the ideal of romance, believing that change is possible and all problems can be resolved by love itself. He believes so strongly in the potential of individuals and the power of love that his romantic ideal can obscure his reason.

INFP's are tempestuous seekers of romance and defenders of truth and beauty. They are devoted and loyal to love and romance is vital to them. They fall in love quite easily, quickly, and incurably. There is certitude in their romantic aspirations that tell the world nothing is of greater importance than affairs of the heart. The interesting aspect of their romantic longing is that their anticipation of love can be a greater pleasure for them than the actual experience of romantic partnership itself. So exhilarated are they by the prospect of love that they fear its manifestation may endanger the flawless anticipation of it! In fact, anticipation of anything pleasurable or joyful excites the INFP's enormously. The eve of an event, the night before, is the dawning of ideals. It is the time of sweet anticipation that romantics adore. Love relationships can often prove to be illusory; they can never quite sustain the same measure of excitement as eager anticipation. Falling in love, for the INFP, is life's greatest adventure.

The interests of Idealists, like the INFP's, are testament to their love of romance. Lilting phrases of poetry and prose appeal to them; fantasies of prince and princess delight them. What is mythical, magical, mystical, or musical is regarded fondly. They are charmed by soft lighting, flowers, and cozy places. Their homes have romantic elements, whatever their style of décor or fashion. Their house is a home in which people feel relaxed, welcome and comfortable. They enjoy nooks for conversation, study, or hobbies and are averse to extremes of color or design that are hard on the eyes. There are blends and combinations of textures and materials in their homes. They are experts at bringing assorted elements together, such as transforming a discarded item into something beautiful or pairing articles of contrast like leather and lace. This is the romantic's unique design—the union, the coming together; it is symbolic of his romantic energy seeking holism.

When dating, the Romantic hero is more at ease in a quiet restaurant or any place where he can spend time getting to know a person new to him. Taking an Idealist to a football game on a first date is probably not a good idea because it's too noisy and impersonal. The INFP tends to form his impressions early in relationships. To him, it's the whole purpose of the first encounter--to get a glimpse of a person's true self. He may surprise his date by revealing rather personal information about himself quite freely. He doesn't enjoy small talk in the least and probably is not up on current events. But, being insightful and intelligent, he knows instinctively if his date is right for him. Hopefully, he will follow his instincts regarding the suitability of a prospective partner, however, that is not always the case.

His romantic quest can sometimes overpower his rationality. As a consequence, the INFP romantic will often stay in incompatible relationships for too long. Perhaps this occurs because separation conflicts with his value for wholeness. Perhaps it is because he is compelled to heal what is broken. Maybe it is due to his fear of loneliness or his inability to hurt another's feelings. It could well be an avoidance of guilt or all of the reasons combined. He needs to feel closely united to a partner and he tends to hang on to broken relationships, remaining hopeful for the resolution of conflict in time. The INFP is definitely a romantic, without question, however, it does not necessarily follow that he is always happy in his relationships for he often is not.

If in a bad relationship, he hangs on until the bitter end, sometimes, abruptly deciding at the oddest moment that it is over. The INFP holds on to love and its possibility until the lack of it becomes intolerable or threatens his health before making a move toward the separation he'll regret so deeply. With or without efforts to restore a failed partnership, the INFP suffers dearly from separation. A the rigidity of a judging type obsessed with order who constantly points out to him how things ought to be done. The judging type may annoy him to no end, however, the INFP wouldn't dream of suggesting that a person change his preference. Furthermore, his intuition probably tells him it can't be done anyway, so there's no point. A mature INFP learns the skill of asserting himself and finding common ground in relationships where difference becomes intolerable. For example, he may learn the need to assert himself when his partnership requires extroverted activities that fail to allow him time alone. He is also a skilled mediator who tends to resolve matters by finding a balance between his own preference and that of others.

It is important for the romantic INFP to feel that his needs are respected by his partner. In a marriage, the Romantic who does not have a connection of intimacy on all levels, including that of the soul, as well as the body and mind, finds himself yielding too much. He will abide an expressive partner's needs by attending social functions when he'd rather curl up with a good book. He might agonizingly listen to his thinking partner's pontifications for hours on end without complaint. Even opposite types can get along together when there is respect, openness, and objectivity. However, if he chronically accommodates without having his own needs validated, he breaks. To avoid problems of this kind, he needs to learn how to communicate his needs to his partner and this becomes easier when he understands his type and his idiosyncrasies.

Romantic attraction can be a mysterious phenomenon. Much has been written about compatibility of the types—which types attract or repel, and so on. Whatever the type he chooses in romance, the INFP needs to feel his values are appreciated and respected by his partner. He also needs recognition of his dedication to those values. Searching for the right personality by type may prove successful; however, it is also important to learn from the experience of being together if someone is worthy of being the soul mate the INFP needs. Paired with another idealist would prove compatible in the area of sharing ideas and intimacy and feeling valued. Idealists thrive on closeness and romance in their love relationships. On the topic of compatibility, Keirsey claimed that Idealists look for soulmates for partners. Their expectations can become disappointing if they are paired with those who enjoy the company of a playmate, a mindmate, or a helpmate as in the case of Keirsey's Artisans, Rationals, and Guardians, respectively. The Romantic wants the one with whom he may share his ideals. He wants closeness on all levels and tenderness and appreciation for his sensitivity. He may find that a fellow INFP is a compatible partner with whom he can share his dreams and plans. However, an INFP couple may also have difficulties with problem solving or decision making because their combined, weaker preferences may not be constructive when it comes to managing major life situations or making important decisions.

There must be harmony in the INFP household and he will strive to achieve that balance. He must feel closely connected to his children at every stage of their lives, supporting them well into their adulthood. Cutting the apron strings is not a requirement for an INFP parent. If his mate does not share his values regarding the rearing of children, there will be problems. INFP's are not averse to allowing their child freedoms, for example, and that view is not held by all types. In an INFP's opinion, one can never love and support a child enough, no matter what. Many an INFP would claim that their children are their greatest gifts, their greatest challenge, their greatest joy or even their very purpose in life. The Romantic hero whose partner shares his unconditional love of their children finds fulfillment in the relationship at a deeply rewarding level. A discussion regarding the INFP's parenting values is important when planning a family to ensure that a partner shares his commitment and dedicated approach to child-rearing.

The Romantic Hero is devoted to important causes and he takes them seriously. The level of devotion the INFP aspires to in both his work and his family life can pose problems, however. There is only so much of his energy to go around. If his obligations outside the family or for the children take precedence, he may be faced with resentment from his partner. If the Romantic's marital allegiance ever comes into question, he'll keep the peace by selflessly giving even more of himself to everything and everyone, possibly wearing himself down and feeling miserable in the process. He may also become indignant at the accusation of his disloyalty. The INFP struggles with the commitments important to him. In the giving of his time to family, friends, church, staff or co-workers, the lines of obligation to each can become muddled to the extent that he may even be unable to prioritize his duties. This degree of selflessness may prove to be a significant problem in his relationships. There are so many causes, so many in need of him, and so much to give. The balance of his benevolence is important. He must choose his obligations to others with a respect for himself if he is to avoid exhaustion and the offense of his loved ones.

For the INFP, all you need is love. A separation from love, even in difficult relationships, is a critical illness for the INFP Healer. A failed marriage, even if inevitably doomed, is incompatible with his fundamental need for wholeness. Recovery is difficult for him when separation occurs. Even geographical distance from loved ones is regrettable and depressing for him. Without the comfort of close human relations and romantic ideals, an INFP can be lost. Without a soulmate for a companion, his rich inner world cannot sustain the degree of advocate, he guides the union of divided parts and people. He has the ability of making things whole because his intuitive perception allows him to examine far more than the objective findings of a situation and to take into account many potentialities. He seeks the ideal of wholeness when he solves a problem by considering all the relevant, unseen factors pertaining to the situation. He never applies the simple and temporary band aid solution or quick fix.

The healing nature of the INFP is akin to that of caregivers in the health professions. Yet, ironically, the Healers are not always happy working in conventional health care roles. In the health care business, the true elements of healing—spending time with patients, communicating with them and educating them, supporting their families and individualizing their treatment is often impossible due to complex bureaucracy, regulatory obligations and hectic schedules. The potential risk to patients due to medical errors is also an unfortunate reality that a Healer cannot abide in traditional health care systems. Adherence to the bioethical principle of "First, do no harm", an INFP imperative, has unfortunately become less prevalent in health care institutions today. Therefore, the healing role of the INFP is not necessarily that of the traditional nurse, physician, or other caregiver in today's health care arenas. If not within actual hospital walls, however, the healing capacity of the INFP's is demonstrated wherever they can make wholeness out of what is broken. Their cause involves mending that which is conflicted, suffering, or disadvantaged.

One who gleans a conceptual awareness of the holistic view appears to be distanced from the reality of a situation. In a crisis, he may appear calm, distracted, or aloof. What is probably happening is that he regards the gravity of the situation differently and his intuition has determined that the situation is not as serious as it may appear to others. People may think he doesn't care, or that he doesn't have a true grasp of the situation, but his intuition has probably told him otherwise--that this too shall pass. This level of insight is a bonus for the INFP, but it is often deemed an enigmatic response by others unlike him. In times of crisis, he may also appear aloof because of his awareness that the history of inhumanity has repeated itself yet again, and there is still so much healing work to be done. When there is a crisis the INFP believes is real and treatable, however, he bolts into action with amazing energy in the face of adversity, like a Romantic Hero.

No matter how many crises he encounters, the INFP holds fast to a singular principle—that of individualism. The importance of the self is central to his theoretical view of holistic health. To him, one's self-awareness is the key to understanding the strife of the world. The healing of an individual's inner conflict is the first stage of healing all conflict. He believes in love as the healing quality that has the power to save the world. Although he may not study every fact on the news regarding the latest pandemic, war, or corruption, he will certainly uphold his personal theory regarding its origins and the reasons for any type of assault upon the human condition. His sense of healing transcends the boundaries of research labs and hospital walls. The more distant the vantage point from which he studies a crisis, the clearer his picture of its nature, its cause, and its cure.

The INFP is hopeful in the face of strife because he believes that man's true goodness is masked by the insecurity created by his own ignorance and fear. He's not fond of all the details of history. He won't have all the facts. Politics and history are probably not among his interests. He's likely not even fond of watching or reading the news. However, he is a pacifist who believes in diplomatic solutions. Without a compassionate spirit, he would be bereft of such weighty aspirations as the healing of separations. He tends to those who need him for comfort and to provide whatever he can to ease the burden and promote healing whether it is an emotional, physical, psychological or spiritual problem. He enjoys helping people reach their full potential. At work, he celebrates the achievement of others. As a leader, he is likely to praise his staff often and provide opportunities in which they grow, even at the expense of reaching his own goals. His interest stems from a true concern for people, their happiness, stability, and health as individuals. He knows the world will never become safe and secure in the presence of emotional insecurity for that is the cause of all controversy.

INFP's just know things. Their keen intuitive awareness is the perfect complement to their compassionate, healing nature. Their interest in the welfare of others takes the lead and their intuition makes the assessment with a perspective that is broad in scope. From that view, they are able to identify similarities and variances, to combine abstract principles, and to create a central theory of everything, the INFP a priori of man's existence. How could an INFP ever deny his healing instinct? It isn't a sixth sense or a psychic awareness, although that may be the case for some. It is more of an intuitive knowing. He just knows that something is so.

His own self-esteem is based on the extent to which his actions have proven to be compassionate. When the INFP learns that his confidence stems from being true to the principles of compassion that he honors, he understands that his worth is enormous. He learns that the high expectations he holds for being fair and kind can lead him to opportunities in which those prospects may be realized. When afforded the opportunity to use his sympathy productively, his self-esteem improves. He may not be aware of how deeply separations affect him. When he defines the separation that he may heal, he finds his purpose. He may become aware that his compassion is not only the source of his healing aptitude and an employable asset; it is medicine for his sense of self-worth.

He is pretty special, for sure. But, at times, the INFP may be very difficult to be around. His outbursts, uncommon as they are, can shatter the nerves of those near him. Never really wanting to hurt anyone, it is clear that there is something seriously wrong when an INFP explodes. And when he snaps, he hardly appears compassionate. Of course, there can be many reasons for these passive-aggressive explosions. Sometimes, the Healer is sick from self-sacrifice. However, a rare INFP outburst is probably the culmination of long-standing tolerance. In either case, his bitterness boils over because he has yielded too much in order to avoid conflict or to mend something broken. The INFP whose anger is released in emotional outbursts has been repressing his natural aggression. He never rocks the boat; he is not particularly assertive, as a rule. Selflessness, keeping the peace, lenience and forbearance involve, to some extent, the suppression of natural aggression and that is not healthy for any type. His outburst is a subconscious release that is an involuntary restoration of his psychic health, however, he typically regrets such overt behavior and feels badly. What he must learn from these episodes is that, on some level, he has suppressed his natural cravings and must nurture them by setting them free.

A possible cause of the Healer's outburst is related to persona. Personas for the INFP take many forms. They are harmful when characterized by yielding reluctantly either too much or for too long in situations that make him behave unlike himself for the sake of something external to him. If an INFP finds himself sacrificing too much by doing work he dislikes, being pushed around, being ignored, or playing along without protest, he needs to wake up to his soul's cries for help. He must learn to allow his aggression an outlet to release his anger by speaking up for himself, by saying no when he means no, and letting others know his feelings about what disturbs him. When he learns to stop holding back for the sake of peace-keeping or compliance, and respect his integrity, the outbursts no longer emerge. If a person is offended during an INFP outburst, the INFP will feel intense guilt and regret for his actions. An emotional outburst, however, is a warning sign of the need for him to let go of blocked energy. His consideration and his avoidance of conflict can make him suppress the natural tendency to assert himself, defend himself or to protest when he feels the need to. Without a release of this emotional tension, he risks the outbursts which he will inevitably find regrettable.

The Healer is far more forgiving of others than he is of himself. An INFP can overlook the flaws of someone's character because he is looking for the gem within the individual, that spark of goodness. It is there, at the root of every human being and uncovering that treasure is important to him. Knowing that underneath one's hurtfulness is one's truth, is what makes a seemingly underserving person worthy of his kindness. He is hopeful of the resurgence of that goodness in time, its re-entry into the personality. To the Healers, a scornful individual is a soul in need of healing. This is how the holistic approach works with the INFP. He can overlook offensive behavior in search of its cause, define that cause, and seek a remedy. He must recognize the need to allow an effective outlet for his own aggression as a means of healing himself as well.

The INFP child developing the benevolent nature is the one in school who stands up for the underdog. He feels sorry for kids who are treated badly, teased, or bullied. He is eager to please his teachers, often studying diligently and being obedient. The INFP parent will not judge his children nor discipline them harshly. Given the vital importance he places on nurturing and allowing a child to develop according to his individuality, he will allow his children the most freedom possible. The INFP's household may resemble a Montessori-style classroom of creative and educational games that allow his children the option to select that which appeals to them. The children will take precedence when it comes to holidays and excursions. Deciphering the true nature of the children he raises will be one of his life's greatest pleasures. And what could be more important to the Advocate than being responsible for the healthy growth and development of his own child? Needless to say, the INFP's make wonderful parents. They are thoughtful, loving and kind. No matter what trouble the child gets himself into— the INFP parent is unwavering in his hopefulness and supportive parenting style.

Feeling, perceiving types are completely devoted to their kids. They are lenient and not likely to regret that forbearance. They marvel at how their children develop, opening their worlds to creative expression and individuality. They make every effort to provide a harmonious environment within which the child grows to know his true self and respect it, to understand the creature he is uniquely born to be. For Advocates, the essence of parenting is the ability to create opportunities for the child that will provide positive experiences. It can be an INFP's greatest pleasure in life. It comes as no surprise that the authors of The Little Prince, Winnie the Pooh, Harry Potter, The Chronicles of Narnia, The Lord of the Rings, The Emperor's New Clothes, and The Ugly Duckling are considered to have been or are imaginative INFP's.

It is a hard lesson for the INFP to learn that his altruism is not always shared by those close to him. If anyone must criticize around the INFP, they had best find an inanimate object or system, because criticism feels like severe punishment to the Healer. He does not take criticism well at all. He may not remember where he

efficiency. Management should either have the facility to resolve its own issues or elicit the input of those within the company who do.

If promoted to a position of authority, engaging in activities at the management level that are designed to correct the mistakes resulting from the business failures of a company is one of the most dreaded responsibilities one could assign to an INFP, especially if his ideas for prevention of the said disaster were never heeded. And this can happen frequently. The protest of an INFP under such circumstances is one of the many contradictory aspects of his nature. When his ideas are too ignored for too long, he explodes in opposition. He does so because he is truly hurting. Having what he treasures most being ignored or undervalued and then making him fix the problems his ideas could have prevented is very painful for an INFP. He will never fake compliance when his values have been assaulted to this degree. Authenticity is too critical to him. He may leave the job and become a writer, a counselor, a minister, or a teacher, where he may have the opportunity to convey with passion what he has learned from the process in order to save his soul.

Postponement is in the middle of virtually every organizational project that is assigned to employees at the management level of corporations. Of course, the INFP does not postpone his own projects; he eagerly submits his work on time in response to a request. He is a diligent worker and he likes to get things done so that he may move on to the next thing. But, at work, he must wait--for responses, approvals, legal reviews, rejections and more meetings until, finally, the delays force him to put the work aside. Delays are not easy for an INFP to reconcile. If a job is important initially, why isn't it important now, he may ask. Either something is truly important or it is not. Dutifully, the INFP lowers his work standard, and, in doing so, becomes accustomed to the abandonment of his assignments and a confusion about what really does constitute value in the company he works for.

In every company in the United States, its employees are required by laws or internal policies to be compliant with rules. Some of them are ridiculous, as everyone knows. The INFP cannot bear senseless regulations because, of course, they lack meaning. Although he is compliant with the rules, he despises many of them and simply must learn to tolerate the ubiquitous restrictions enforced upon him. It is a hindrance for the INFP to comply with meaningless rules. His coworkers may go along without complaint, but the INFP must argue against rules lacking validity. Hopefully, he does so quietly. However, he will have those strong opinions for change and he will express opposing views where others fear to tread. If he is told there is already a mechanism for addressing the problem, and the initiative is one of those flavor-of-the-month theories borrowed from the latest management seminar, the INFP risks a stress-induced illness worthy of a leave of absence.

The INFP doesn't have a work routine. He works in a myriad of ways and no two days will be the same, if he can help it, no matter how repetitive his job may be. He may vary his daily tasks in terms of their timing, operational steps, and duration. Of course, he will create many lists and will get his work done on time, but he doesn't follow a set routine, not even for lunch. *Do this* or *do that* are antagonistic phrases in an INFP's life, sort of like perpetually buzzing alarm clocks. He doesn't like the idea of structured activities. He is not always punctual and he may not even be totally prepared for meetings and presentations. Winging it was made for the perceiving types. Disorder is his order and if he *is* organized, he has probably learned to be as a matter of compliance in his situation at work or due to the influence of a Rational in his personal life. Of course, tardiness results in all kinds of problems at school and at work, but the Romantic Hero would rather be creative and free to conduct himself as he pleases than to be micromanaged. It is another of his contradictions that the INFP is obedient at work, yet hates to be dictated to.

It is a shame that idealists are not more valued in business. Their gifts of perception could help companies succeed. The Healer could be just the right choice of business partner or executive. As leaders, the INFP's advocate for their employees. They respect the needs of the people and can restructure any organizational chart, by placing people exactly where they are best suited. They can identify where company mission is most egregiously breached and prioritize the corrections necessary. They can identify risks that threaten the company's resources. They will be the last to recommend bureaucratic solutions that plague employees. Every time they are assigned a project that lacks importance, every meeting that fails to address the agenda, every wasted effort, for them, is pure torture. They would rather redecorate their offices than do busywork. They would rather take a walk than read one more email in a trail of monotonous, repetitive discussions. They would rather make a coffee run than attend a meeting that has had the same, unresolved topic on its agenda for the past year.

The INFP does not accept mediocrity. He is devoted to the production of quality work, sometimes to the point of exhaustion, even if his job satisfaction is in the dumps, because he is principled. The family at home may have to bear his constant wailing because an INFP's sense of value is too great for most business climates unless he is the sole proprietor. He asks why all the time. Why was this meeting called? Why was this person chosen to lead this department? Why did the company invest in that or not address this problem? Unfortunately, his questions are either unanswered or stifled, or he receives criticism for his negativity. How one's recommendation for improvement or for risk prevention could be considered negative is beyond him.

The Romantic Hero, however, must adapt and perhaps due to his rare constitution, he is highly flexible and versatile. The "hard skills" that embellish his resume are testament to his adaptability. He learns new skills readily to the extent that he may be mistaken for a more analytical type. The INFP is actually quite suited to work that involves data analysis. This capacity may be attributed to his ability to see the big picture and to identify patterns and abstract associations. He is excellent at the dissemination of information for reporting data and analyzing trends, especially if the goal involves something he values and is not a full-time responsibility. Development of his less-practiced functions, as for all the personality types, broadens his skills and employability. Jobs involving the aggregation of data that entail the use of statistics, programming, or accounting may not be suitable, however, research may appeal to him in the areas of his interests. Most careers provide opportunities for trending data to some extent. The Romantic's preference for the ministry, psychology, psychiatry, social work, music, counseling, teaching, and, of course, writing are just a few and quite suitable careers for the INFP in which data may be analyzed. As long as it isn't called *data mining* or *informatics*, an INFP may find a great deal of interest in working with a limited amount of statistical data.

Many jobs keep the INFP from sharing his natural gifts with the world because it isn't easy for him to find meaningful work that meets his standards. If unable to enjoy the ideal type of work, the kind most suitable, an INFP would do well to at least seek employment with companies that support his need for a respectful environment. In the right career, if allowed the independence that makes him flourish, he will do wonders and with amazing speed and quality. He will eagerly share his suggestions for improvement and change, without a doubt. Even if the INFP is in a line of work unsuited to him, for the right cause, he will learn the skills required in order to perform well because he truly wants to do well. When the work assigned to him or managed by him is for a worthy cause, his energy and enthusiasm are outstanding and he works industriously. If micromanaged, he is dejected. A self-employed INFP or one who shares a working partnership with a personality that complements his type is certainly at an advantage because working for people tends to be challenging for him on too many levels.

Since he does his best when independent of others, he is more fulfilled in careers that provide resources for his independent work style. On the other hand, his independent nature also causes problems for him when he fails to obtain the help he needs to accomplish his goals, perhaps help with matters in the area of logistics and finance which do not typically appeal to him. Since he is a loner, he sometimes misses opportunities for aligning with the right resources that can improve his progress. Despite this disadvantage, independent work is his distinct preference. He loves the company of a few close friends and acquaintances but also needs his freedom and independence. In fact, the INFP employee can accomplish more in in one day on his own than some of his gregarious colleagues accomplish in several, if he is allowed his to work uninterrupted.

The world needs dreamers who challenge the status quo, and encourage others to seek a better place. The INFP has no desire for power or control, which is why he is not often found in the upper ranks of corporations. The thrill, for him, is hypothesizing in the world of possibilities. Anyone with an INFP in their group benefits from his enthusiasm and his insights. He may screw up on some of the facts and you may point this out to him, but unless it is a serious mistake (unlikely) he will hold firm with his stance. And that stance will change too as necessary. He will revise his idea long before the group is aware the change is needed. These INFP traits are strengths that are undervalued in the corporate arena. There are many places, however, in which his ideas may thrive.

The artistic, counseling, teaching, and writing careers to which he is drawn provide opportunities for the privacy and independent thinking the INFP craves. These are not always lucrative careers, however, money is not high on the INFP's list of needs. In the world of creative expression he has less bureaucracy to deal with, fewer rules, less mundane busywork, and greater freedom to achieve meaning and purpose. There, in his quiet independent place, his mind is the idea engine it should be. There, he learns that the world needs dreamers and that it's okay to want to be alone because miraculous ideas are spawned in quiet places. Independently, the INFP is free to spill the ideas in his heart onto the canvas, the music sheet, the writing paper, or with a client in need. There alone, he is romantic, lyrical, expressive, and creative. Working alone or with small groups of people whom he can help in some way is where the INFP is at his best.

The INFP's choice of study is not necessarily limited to fine art and the humanities. The programs of study that combine disciplines were made for the INFP. The Healer excels at making associations and combinations out of complex and diverse concepts to arrive at something groundbreaking. His talents may not be those of the artisan, the inventor, or the rational, but given the opportunity, the INFP is indeed an innovator whose perspectives are demonstrated with exceptional creativity. As already mentioned, he may enjoy Interdisciplinary Studies programs where diversely different courses may be combined such as a science with fine art or a language with psychology. The Idealist enjoys combining diverse principles. He does not, however, require a course in innovation in order to do so.

Human Resources may be a suitable place for him if recruitment, retention, or counseling of staff is involved. There, he can be true to form, because the INFP is a natural for helping people be where they are best suited and where they may achieve their greatest satisfaction. Of course, careers that involve writing or scholarly pursuits in general appeal to him as well. Repetitive work, and particularly mundane work, is no type of employment for the INFP. He cannot just go through the motions without significant emotional damage.

There are many alternative approaches for the INFP to incorporate both strong and less-developed personality aspects at work. He may dislike dealing with insurance policies or contracts, for example. However, he may be interested in helping people purchase insurance plans or advocate for them by handling their insurance claims. He may even be adept at crunching numbers that demonstrate trends in an enterprise to objectify what his intuition suspects is true about an aspect of an industry—as long as it involves people to some extent. In fact, he is interested in work that involves the combination of many talents, as long as his natural talents are applied. He is unlikely to enjoy accounting as an occupation, for example, because there is no allure for the subjective or the abstract. Still, he is quite capable of using accounting to some extent in work that is more suitable to him. He can certainly learn to balance a budget or master a database application as long as he is not required to do it all day, every day.

The Healer is keenly aware of the negative impact of stressful work on people. He is an advocate for employee rights and he knows full well that if work feels more like bondage, there will be serious repercussions in terms of one's health. Oppressive or unsafe work conditions are intolerable for the Romantic Hero. If he is truly miserable with his job, he needs to find a place where he can make a difference. He must heal something somewhere. If he finds his place, he may then be his authentic self and have the freedom to do what he loves. It is vital for the INFP who must work for a living, to find work that is meaningful, work that has purpose and when he does, he is free.

There is something to heal for every single INFP. If he struggles with finding suitable work, he might consider opportunities for using his natural, holistic talents. What does he care to heal becomes the question, rather than what kind of job should he consider. He might ask himself what it is he wishes to make whole--what is broken, sick, or disturbed. Is it broken hearts or broken dreams? He may consider what sickness he can tend to—that of flowers or plants, perhaps. Would he do better mending emotional separations as a counselor of some kind? Does he feel the need for healing illiteracy or any lack of education? Are his deepest feelings of benevolence for infants, children, teenagers, adults, or older people? How many does he plan to heal? Can he heal millions with his written words, his songs, his prayers, or his talents? He is probably a dedicated worker who has proven himself and won the respect of his supervisors in his career. If, however, he is not gratified with the type of work he is doing, he may simply need to find something he can help restore to health and the resources to do so. Like most people, the INFP may take some wrong occupational turns before he finds his ideal vocation, but he may rest assured that his vision of holism in some profession or role will be most rewarding.

doors to seeing his dreams come true by removing the yoke of his diminished sense of self-worth. The Romantic Healers can suffer from self-doubt more than other types. Setting high moral standards of behavior contributes to this problem because it is difficult to consistently maintain ideals. The INFP may feel that failure to achieve some of his ambitions is due to his personal limitations. However, quite often, his self-doubts are actually misperceptions. He has a tendency to underestimate his gifts. If an INFP has feelings of inadequacy, he must stop berating himself. He must lose the idea of others outside himself probably being right and recognize that if he feels that way, it is a serious sign of self-doubt that must be remedied.

First of all, the requirement for the INFP is to *know* the ideal, not to *be* the ideal. If he wants to feel better about himself, he must embrace the idea of the shade flower as an image of great beauty, not a forlorn, impoverished waif. Feeling victimized can be common for the INFP. In actual fact, the INFP's are special, exquisite, rare, truthful, loyal, and dependable. These attributes are strengths, not weaknesses. When he learns to enjoy and treasure his mind's wanderlust, his changing interests, his messy desk, his indecisions, his outbursts, his weeks on the couch, his erratic diet, his lack of routine, his tardiness, his sweetness, his humanitarianism, and his politeness, he might just realize how truly wonderful he is. He must love it all and allow it all to be, the good, the bad, and the ugly. There is no way to celebrate life unless one can celebrate the self completely with all its flaws included. Happiness does not come to those who are so hard on themselves that they develop a self-image of scarcity. Learning to admit to imperfection as the norm and allowing the imperfections to be is the ideal. Believing in one's shortcomings as ruinous is not.

The Healer must heal himself, especially if he is inflicted with the wounds of regret. Perhaps he cannot stop the replay of a mistake in his memory. To heal himself of guilt, it is helpful to consider what his Healer self was up to at the time he made the so-called mistake. In the case of the Healer, it is quite possible that a Romantic hero's type of cause led him to make a certain choice, right or wrong. Moreover, it is equally possible that the choice was made while the Healer was in disguise, wearing a socially-required mask of persona. The fact remains, it makes no difference. All that matters is that the event occurred. Period. The reasons for making the choices he made were probably multitudinous. What matters now is what he believes about himself and it is surely a misperception, if he still agonizes over regrettable life choices. To rid himself of regrets for making unsound decisions, hurting someone's feelings inadvertently, or missing an opportunity, he needs only to consider what the experience provided for his growth. Identifying what one learns from a bad experience turns self-blame into opportunity. How wonderful life can be when it is possible to feel grateful for the opportunity a bad situation provided.

It is easier said than done to consider mistakes as opportunities, but they are. If the INFP focuses on past errors or any misgivings, he can stand back from them by painting one of his big pictures. Seeing a life journey from afar, as if in a picture that maps his life path in his mind or on paper takes his focus away from the hurdles and places them where they belong in the overall picture. When able to focus on lessons learned in the big picture of a life by visualizing a metaphorical image, the rationale for decisions becomes apparent and the ups and downs become the necessary steps along the way. An INFP can paint the picture of his life's journey by imagining it as a story in a film. In this film, he is the main character, complete with all the many costumes he has worn, the scenes he has visited, and the characters he has met. With imagery, he is capable of healing his self-doubts by changing his focus and looking through a different lens, one that views the relevant aspects of his past as a uniquely divined journey rather than a lost cause. He turns his focus to that which is valid and purposeful when his life is depicted as a progression of moments, one leading to the next and one of a story where the ruts were merely temporary obstacles from which he climbed out and moved on.

When seen from a distance in this manner, a life journey's positive elements emerge. An INFP will, no doubt, examine aspects of his beautiful type in action and understand that the so-called mistakes were the traps, the detours and the obstacles that simply and necessarily caused him to wander off the road for something better. He may say that romance turned out badly because he was simply being a hopeless romantic in search of love. In so doing, he may have learned to focus on the good times and to appreciate his love of romance. He may say a failed business venture was the result of holding fast to an ideal that couldn't be found, rather than berating himself for lack of business prowess. He may see his jealousies as the result of an eternal lack of self-worth that pervaded many years unnecessarily and discover that he inherited a belief of his low self-worth from childhood experiences and that belief may now change.

The big picture of an INFP's life may reveal that the Healer at some points along the journey lost his ability to thrive entirely. That dark period of his life, viewed from a new perspective, one in which he remembers what healed his sorrows, can be seen as a valuable time in his history for which he may feel immense gratitude instead of remorse. INFP's are able to create such imagery and would do well to use it therapeutically if they suffer from guilt feelings. The Healer's journey, put into perspective in this manner, reveals an INFP's unique call to be the Healer at some level. The "mistakes" along the way become external to his mother, the wise old woman and the wise old man, to name a few. These motifs are universal and ageless archetypes that represent vital aspects of human life. The motifs are dramatized in unique ways, depending on the dreamer's personal experience. The dreamer's subconscious becomes the director, so to speak, commanding the stage. The dream performance is completely unrestricted by the thoughts or emotions of the conscious self. As the conscious mind sleeps, the subconscious mind takes the stage, uncensored and unchallenged. The subconscious mind, unimpeded by the ego or consciousness portrays what the dreamer needs to know in order to compensate for an imbalance of his psyche. The subconscious is a barometer of psychic health and it knows what, when, and how to communicate with the dreamer. If invited, the subconscious will surely visit and provide answers for the dreamer who requests them. Dreams are non-judgmental and they are never forced upon the dreamer. They provide dramatic depictions of one's reality and their appearance summons the dreamer to pay heed to some aspect of the personality that needs adjustment.

Although some dreams are reruns of the day's activities, much the same as a child's dream of having been to a picnic earlier in the day, for the adult, dreams are symbols of maladies, particularly those the dreamer needs to be aware of. For example, the dreamer may be jealous of someone's success or may truly dislike a person in his actual life. To his surprise, the disliked person features in a dream as a beloved close friend or even a sexual partner. Dreams of this nature often urge the dreamer to look at what is despised about the person, what Jung called the Shadow self. The dream is urging the dreamer to incorporate the same Shadow aspect into his own personality to some degree. The disliked person is adored and unthreatening in the dream because what is loathed by the dreamer needs to be incorporated to some extent into his own personality. Dreams of this nature may be astonishing, perhaps, but they are relevant. The Shadow is the undeveloped, opposite aspect that balances the personality. It is represented in dreams as various dark symbols that urge the dreamer to reconcile his undeveloped self.

Only the dreamer is truly capable of determining the meaning of his dreams. However, it isn't always necessary to read too much into them or to have the insights of a psychiatrist to interpret their meaning. Sometimes, dream messages are obvious. If a dreamer is swarmed by bees, for example, he may well think about what's bugging him. If he feels smothered by someone in his dream, it is probable that the person in the dream is figuratively smothering the life out of the dreamer in reality. Lovely feelings of floating, levitating, or flying, are suggestions to lighten up, to have fun, or to find freedom or pleasure. Good-feeling dreams from which one reluctantly awakens are gifts of pure pleasure, delivered when needed. They give the dreamer a taste of what may be lacking in his life. An astute INFP, who works too hard, might simply be advised that he needs to relax or to take things less seriously. Pleasure in dreams may point to the lack of it in one's life and the need to find it somewhere because it feels so good. When climbing and unable to reach a summit, the dream may be revealing that the pursuit of a certain goal has become too demanding. The extent to which a dream implores the dreamer to take heed is the indication of the urgency of the problem depicted. A loud voice, a sudden flash of light, a single word, a scream, or even sublime silence in a dream pleads the dreamer to pay heed to something important.

Failure will also figure in dreams, containing symbols unique to the dreamer's personal circumstances and experience. The people or the scene will vary, but the feeling of failure invoked by a dream—the shame, the embarrassment, or fear, will be there. If the dream is a recurring one, the reason is obvious--the problem itself is a recurring one and is yet unresolved. The failure dream surfaces in the form of incomplete tasks, vulnerability, being scorned, or by the presence of figures of authority. These are the direct messages of feelings of unworthiness; they may be interpreted only by the dreamer who must examine the feelings the dream evokes and his personal attitudes toward the symbols depicted.

Dreams are rhetorical messages that combine motifs common to man with symbols that are relevant for the dreamer. Death of a relative, for example, could be symbolic of a situation *about* the relative that must die within the dreamer, perhaps the fear or guilt associated with him. The lessons of dreams are kind and compassionate, vivid perhaps, but not disparaging. Dreams appear to provide direction regarding the emotional and psychological state of the self and what the dreamer needs to know to in order to achieve greater stability and happiness. Chaos, disaster, catastrophe, confusion, are obvious messages of the disruptive influences of life situations for the dreamer. They could be warnings of the need to release pent up aggression or tension. These unsettling dreams may remain in the memory for some time, even in the wakeful state, and they are intended to do so. Their purpose is to demand attention to the state of a situation and the need to take action to achieve balance. When the dreamer dissects the parts of a dream he reveals wisdom from his true self, the part of his being that is unaltered by a circumstance, problem, or neurotic tendency.

The analysis of dreams is a highly subjective process. The dream conveys its message through much more than its symbols or even its overall story, fragmented and indecipherable as it can be. Its characteristic levels of sensual intensity—its volume, color, focus, and tone, have significance as well. The response or how the dream makes the dreamer feel is the best indicator of its meaning. Dreams are eloquent metaphors. For an INFP, they can be an easy study. What could be better than to analyze metaphors pertaining to the true self? In fact, an INFP's intuitive nature and need for self-awareness predispose him to being a dream *expert*. When he is aware that his true self is revealed in his dreams, he may become an avid student, eager to learn what he needs to know about living a more integrated and successful life.

Some Healers suffer from suppressed feelings that cause blockages of energy needing a healthy release. Being reserved and polite, harmonious and compliant makes it so for them. However, there is no reward for holding back natural aggression. It is normal and necessary for aggression to be released. There is no truth to the belief that aggression is always violent, although it can be. Non-violent aggressive action can be expressed in many acceptable ways and is the means by which humans release their energies of frustration, confusion, anger and fear. Holding these feelings back leads to psychological and physical ill-health. This type of pressure causes emotional instability and leads to many diseases related to stress. Ironically, if release of natural aggression is avoided for long, it discharges itself in an exaggerated form as the very violent or offensive actions its suppression was intended to control.

Natural aggression is a physiological and psychological human response. It plays an effective role in the maintenance of balanced body chemistry necessary for the prevention of illness and the restoration of health. A newborn's cry is a formidable example of natural aggression. The mechanism of birth itself is another. Yet, despite its purpose as a vital human instinct, natural aggression is widely regarded as an unacceptable behavior and is synonymous with violence. Natural aggression is actually the communication of man's powerful energy in motion. It is the energy of life itself. It is an expressive thrust of natural instinct that communicates man's deepest needs and its intensity varies in relation to those needs. However, it is feared, loathed, condemned and calmed by social, religious, and cultural constraints. These constraints create a demoralization of human nature itself and are the result of hubris and ignorance. Man has assigned an undeserved reputation of vulgarity and lustful abandon to his very essence-- his natural instinct for aggression. In so doing, he creates his guilt, his fear, his longing, and the very animosity he attempts to subdue.

The powerfully strong emotions of romantic love and of sexual release, of protest against cruelty, are expressions of natural aggression. The strict warning for a child to avoid danger is another as is a demand for civil rights, the sobs of grief, and the cries of loneliness. Humans burst into the world with an aggressive force and that force is vital. A baby cries vigorously from hunger in order to be fed. Sexual desire is an aggressive cry for physical pleasure and nothing less than procreation itself. Sobbing and screaming is natural aggression pleading for relief from a lack of love or the loss of it. Love is a powerful form of aggression as well. It does not seep forth from the spirit. It bolts like a flash releasing a powerful surge of human energy. Love is described as passionate, but it is a powerful demonstration of natural aggression. Whether it is aggression, the visceral charge, energy, or passion, the softer term, humans need its release when it is there. The suppression of aggression is a damaging and potentially lethal condition.

Love's expression is strongly aggressive. Love is the ultimate, natural and most powerful expression of mankind because human beings hate that which takes love away. In the tragedy of Romeo and Juliet, the young lovers' deaths heal the longstanding hatred between their families and peace is restored. Such is the power of love. Hate arises against the conditions that deny love's authority, not against the individual bereft of lovingness. When love is threatened or lost, man's aggression emerges. Denying aggressive life energy is unnecessary. Suppressing the inclination to assert oneself, to protest against a wrong, to fulfill an instinctual physical desire, to demand what is vital to life or to a cause, is to stifle the very impetus that gives birth to fulfillment, growth, and happiness. Without an outlet for the expression of natural aggression, it lies dormant, yet its power can never be squelched. It will force its way into existence, for it is pure energy that cannot be diminished. Without a healthy outlet for the expression of natural aggression, it explodes with great force, often when least expected and when it does, there is great damage. Natural aggression is dangerous only if neglected.

To hold back a life force is not only unnecessary, it has no rational requirement, unless the form of aggression is an intentional violation which is always wrong. To incorporate its healthy influence into life is to gain a sense of freedom and enjoyment. It is about claiming for oneself what is one's own. An INFP may harbor feelings of resentment if he gives of himself too much or too often or if his peace-keeping neutrality hides his underlying animosity. His ensuing resentment or anxiety, or perhaps physical pain or loss of energy, are signs of his need to break open the blocked energy of his aggression and set it free. He needn't rage nor accuse, or in any way violate, but he must set it free. He may find alternate forms of communication such as speaking up for himself in truth when he feels taken advantage of or saying "no" when he means no. He can pour his aggressive energy into his work, exercise or hobby. These are acceptable and healing forms of natural aggression.

The INFP who cares for his true self and acknowledges his full potential becomes the great Healer. When he expresses his emotional needs, he avoids self-sabotaging thoughts of weakness. When he values all aspects of his complex personality, he is happy. If he can fully accept his weaknesses as equally as his strengths, his self-respect and confidence is upheld. Trusting his intuitive wisdom provides him with an eternal source of strength. When he allows himself moments in the comfort of his shade garden, he is peaceful. The INFP is a beloved creature. He is a defender of truth and authenticity, a Romantic Hero. He seeks meaning and life purpose with an incomparable drive. He is the great healer of separations. He is humble, forgiving, intelligent, and kind. He is a prophetic dreamer, a futurist, a literary genius. He is a highly principled and ambitious advocate of human potential. His challenge is to value his power and believe in himself. The INFP who finds his healing purpose finds the way to his freedom. And when he does, he makes the world a better place.

Treasure the gifts differing, dear Healers. Invite the world to your gardens in the shade. Never doubt the power of your compassion and your healing spirit. You are here to teach us what you know and the world awaits your message of hope and healing.

Sandra Nichols
Port Saint Lucie, Florida
April, 2016
sandra@sandranichols.net

Other Books by Sandra Rogers

Dead Mentors, a Novel

Change Your Path: Career Alternatives for Hospital Nurses

31911900R00060

Printed in Great Britain
by Amazon